A GOLDEN WHEELS BOOK
CONTEMPORARY CLASSICS
Three Decades of Automotive Milestones

RICH TAYLOR
Photography by TAYLOR-CONSTANTINE

GOLDEN PRESS / NEW YORK
Western Publishing Company, Inc., Racine, Wisconsin

Foreign Cars

Aston Martin DBS
Austin-Healey 100-6
Bentley Hooper R-type
Bentley Mulliner Flying Spur
Citroën SM
Facel II
Ferrari 275 GTB/4
Ferrari 365 GTB/4
Jaguar XK-120
Lancia Aurelia B.20
Lancia Fulvia Sport
Maserati Ghibli
Mercedes-Benz 300 SL
MG TC
Morgan Plus-4
Porsche Speedster
Rolls-Royce Silver Wraith
Triumph 2000
Triumph TR-3B

American Cars

Chevrolet Nomad
Corvette
Camaro
Chrysler Town and Country
Chrysler 300B
Ford Thunderbird
Hudson Super Six
Lincoln Continental Mark II
Packard Caribbean
Packard 400
Shelby GT-350
Shelby Cobra 289
Studebaker Commander Starliner
Studebaker Avanti

Library of Congress Catalog Card Number: 74-77913

Copyright © 1974 by Western Publishing Company, Inc. All rights reserved. Printed in the U.S.A. Golden, a Golden Book® and Golden Press® are trademarks of Western Publishing Company, Inc.

There's a new breed of car collector. The cars he prizes are quality vehicles built during the last thirty years, contemporary classics that are destined to be significant milestones in the history of the automobile. But they're more than just museum pieces. That's the appeal of these cars. While antique and vintage machines are visually exciting and historically important, they're often rather disappointing to drive. The same is true of new cars. Restrictive legislation has taken much of the romance and just plain fun out of driving. But during that special period separating World War II and Ralph Nader, dozens of fine cars were made that are beautiful, exciting, functional and in almost every way better machines than what we have now. And a lot of people are discovering this.

The typical collector who has just bought his first contemporary classic couldn't be happier. And this is only the beginning. If he's like most other enthusiasts, he'll never buy another new car. Not because he can't afford one. But because his classic is a better car than anything he could buy new. It may be ten or twenty years old, but if it's in good condition it can do everything a new car can do, and many things new cars can't.

An old Ferrari 275 GTB/4, for example, costs less than a new full-size American sedan bristling with optional extras. But instead of a depreciating hulk that gobbles gas, is no fun to drive and is about as distinctive as a toaster, the collector has one of the last true handbuilt mechanical masterpieces still available to the man without a fortune to spend. And his Ferrari will become more valuable as time goes on. The exquisite styling will be more and more esteemed as new cars grow safety bumpers and other paraphernalia to meet increasingly strict federal standards. And the performance of his Ferrari—good gas mileage coupled with incredible acceleration and high top speed, not to mention racetrack handling and unbelievably good brakes—is already a mere memory in new cars.

Of course, much the same driving enjoyment is to be found in less puissant collector's cars. The heady joy of an MG TC, burbling along in a state of perpetual youthfulness, is unmatched in the world of present-day automobiles. A Morgan is the same, only more so. Driving one is a contagious mix of noisy, windy, bouncy sport and carefree abandon.

At the opposite extreme from these roadsters are the opulent luxury sedans and limousines whose craftsmanship is not to be

Foreword

found in modern cars. The meticulous handwork of a coachbuilt Rolls would require a price tag of six figures to duplicate today. Even a delightfully dowdy Hudson has a luxury all its own. With the supple suspension soaking up the bumps, the huge engine barely challenged by freeway speeds, and with such small refinements as the old tube-type radio with its big round tones creating a total atmosphere of euphoria, even the most jaded car fancier will find himself transported to another, more genteel age. A Chrysler Town and Country has the same effect, and certainly Packards and Continentals are equally luxurious. Concepts of sport, of enjoyment, of luxury are no longer basic to the building of automobiles. But that isn't to say there aren't many discriminating drivers to whom these factors are still important.

More and more collectors are finding that quality cars built within the last thirty years are the perfect answer to what they require in an automobile. And the range of these cars is broad enough to include almost anything a driver could need. From a lordly Bentley to an unassuming Nomad station wagon, there are

1967 Ferrari 275 GTB/4 / Courtesy Vintage Car Store

collectible classics to fit every preference—and any price range. All are distinguished by their styling, their performance and their craftsmanship. And the fact that they can only appreciate in value.

For most collectors, any one of these qualities would be more than enough to justify purchasing a contemporary classic. But at the very heart of the matter, the decision is subjective. The collector buys the car for the special way he feels when he looks at it. Or the special pride he feels when someone else admires it. Or the satisfaction of being able to go out and drive—really drive, the way cars were meant to be driven—and test himself and his car under the most exciting conditions possible.

He knows why he's a collector, and why he picked his particular car. Because it does something for him. It may not have the same effect on everybody, but that's just the point. Most people are content to be herded along in mundane, identical tin cans. Only a relatively few are perceptive enough to appreciate true merit, to actively seek out cars that are better than they need to be. These people are collectors. And their cars are contemporary classics.□

Aston Martin

Aston Martins are among the most desirable cars in the world, the last word in the development of the British sports car. They're brutal machines with savage performance matched by perfect styling—a rare and sublime combination.

Sir David Brown bought the Aston Martin concern in 1947, along with the venerable firm of Lagonda. His first new car was introduced in 1950. It had a revised Aston frame fitted with a De Dion rear axle and powered by a double overhead cam Six originally designed by W. O. Bentley for Lagonda. The coachwork was very Italian in style—superlative enough to be chosen for an historic Museum of Modern Art design show in 1953—with a distinctive grille that has remained the hallmark of all subsequent Astons. The original 2.6-liter DB2 evolved over the years into the 3.7-liter DB4, in turn becoming the 4.0-liter DB5 and DB6.

The $20,000 DBS was presented in 1968, offered with either the classic Six or a new 5340cc V-8. Like all Astons, the DBS has amazing road-holding, precise steering and crushing acceleration. Top speed is well over 160 mph. And the styling is superb. In every way, it is an overwhelming car, taking its fortunate driver to the very limits of high-speed motoring.

1973 Aston Martin DBS / Courtesy Grossman Motorcar Corporation

1958 Austin-Healey 100-6 / Courtesy Theodore Cryer

Austin-Healey

At the 1952 London Motor Show, former rally star Donald Healey exhibited a sleek little roadster created around Austin A90 sedan components. Austin's management was so impressed by the enthusiastic public reception to this prototype two-seater that production began immediately. Called the Austin-Healey 100-4, the car utilized a 2.6-liter Austin Four to propel it over 100 mph—hence the name. In 1956, the 100-4 received a sturdy Six of the same displacement, and became the 100-6. For 1959, this was enlarged to 2912cc, and eventually developed 150 hp before production of the Austin-Healey 3000 ceased in 1968.

All Austin-Healeys are a supreme blend of solid—virtually indestructible—construction with gorgeous compact lines. The 3-liter cars will easily run 115 mph, and the earlier models are nearly as fast. The handling is classically impeccable, and the engine produces huge bellows of sound and torque. This happy combination sends Healey drivers carving through back roads with euphoric grins on their windblown faces, leaving trails of the envious staring after.

Bentley

Modern Bentleys have nothing in common with the classic juggernauts created by W. O. Bentley during a dozen glorious years ending in 1931, after which Bentley Motors was purchased out of receivership by Rolls-Royce. Since then, Bentleys have been merely modified Rolls-Royces meant to appeal to a sportier driver. The most desirable Rolls/Bentleys are the R-type Continentals built between 1952 and 1955 and the S-type Continentals, which continued until the advent of the Silver Shadow range in 1966.

A total of 208 R-type Continentals were built on the 4566cc and 4887cc Mark VI chassis. Most of these have lightweight, fastback four-passenger coupe bodies by Mulliner, but a very few are different. The 1954 R-type shown here is one of them. It has Hooper touring sedan coachwork, which doesn't allow the 120 mph top speed of the Mulliner, but is far more elegant and luxurious.

1954 Bentley Hooper R-type / Courtesy Charles Gibso

This 1960 S-type Continental by Mulliner, delightfully known as the Flying Spur, is probably the most rewarding of all Rolls/Bentleys. Its engine is a 185 hp, 6230cc aluminum V-8 from the standard Rolls Silver Cloud, but subtle changes in gearing and suspension make it a genuine 120 mph motorcar—with handling to match. Available as either a four-door or a much rarer two-door, the Flying Spur cost over $25,000 new and is still worth more than half that. All Bentleys are authentic classics, but the coachbuilt Continentals are the best—beautiful, dependable, exciting and considerably more puissant than the production-line models.

1960 Bentley Mulliner Flying Spur / Courtesy Fredric M. Kanter

1973 Citroën SM / Courtesy Grossman Motorcar Corporation

Citroën

The Citroën SM is the first French car since the Facel II that can be considered even a minor classic. Built by the fifty-year-old firm of Citroën SA, it's a rare and wonderful vehicle. The engine is a Maserati double overhead camshaft V-6 of only 2670cc. This lightweight jewel is coupled to an unusual 5-speed, front-wheel-drive transaxle, but it also powers a complex and sophisticated hydraulic system that assists everything from the adjustable suspension ride height to the self-centering oval steering wheel.

In some ways, the Citroën SM may be the most complex road car ever built, and for that reason alone it would be remarkable. But it is also blessed with excellent handling and good brakes—and one of the most perfect aerodynamic bodies yet designed. It is primarily this wind-cheating shape that allows the small, 180 hp V-6 to pull the Citroën to a top speed of 140 mph. The subtle aesthetics of the SM make it one of the most sleekly beautiful of modern cars, yet always the functional derivation of the shape is evident.

After fifteen years as a sheet-metal fabricator for automobile manufacturers, Jean Daninos of Facel SA started building his own cars
in 1954. The first of these, a handsome coupe called the Facel Vega,
was powered by an American Chrysler V-8. He progressed from this
to the F.V.S. and the HK-500. These were similar in concept, becoming more and more powerful as the imported Chrysler engines
increased from 276 cubic inches in 1954 to 383 cubic inches in 1961.

The more sophisticated Facel II was introduced in 1962, now with
a curb weight of only 3400 pounds holding down a 390 hp Chrysler.
With a 4-speed transmission, disc brakes and other refinements, the
Facel II is a bona fide 150 mph motorcar. The elegant styling is
superb, from the slim roof pillars to the delicate vertical grille and
subtle treatment of the streamlined headlights. It seems a very Gallic
car, an urbane gentleman's carriage.

The Facel II had a price tag when new in the $12,000 range; it's
still worth around $8000 today. All the Chrysler-powered Facel
coupes are collector's cars, unlike the smaller all-Facel car, the
Facellia, which wrecked the company's perilous finances and led to
the demise of the Facel II in 1964.

Facel

1962 Facel II / Courtesy Fredric M. Kanter

1972 Ferrari 365 GTB/4 / Courtesy Harold Tananbaum

Ferrari

Surely the most desirable of all Ferrari street machines is the 275 GTB. Certainly it is beautiful. And the 3.3-liter, 300 hp V-12 with its six Weber carburetors and single overhead cams (on the GTB) or double overhead cams (on the GTB/4) is a joy to operate, behold and hear—particularly as it approaches the 8000 rpm redline. Top speed is over 165 mph, and for a mere $14,500 between 1964 and 1968, a lucky sport could have one of the great ones. People have been collecting GTBs since they first came out, for it is axiomatic that *any* Ferrari is worth saving. For around $9000, smart money has already snapped up the best 275 GTBs.

But big money is after the 365 GTB/4, known to the world as the Daytona. It cost about $25,000 when introduced to this country in 1969, and used ones have hardly depreciated at all. The exquisite streamlined body is one of Pininfarina's finest designs, and the Scaglietti coachwork is surprisingly sturdy. The engine is a 4390cc version of the ubiquitous Ferrari V-12, and will push the average Daytona to a guaranteed 174 mph right off the used car lot. It's just about the highest-performance car you can buy, and the brakes and handling are more than a match for the engine. Recent emission, safety and energy conservation laws have made the concept of the Daytona impractical, so those who must have the ultimate are already hoarding at least one GTB/4.

1967 Ferrari 275 GTB/4 / Courtesy Vintage Car Store ▶

1953 Jaguar XK-120 / Courtesy Bob Grossman

Jaguar

Sir William Lyons never sold a bad car. A few Jaguars may have been a little less than perfect, but there's not a rotten one in the bunch. Which is a remarkable track record for forty years. Of all those cars, probably the most significant street model is the XK-120. The pre-war SS 100 is certainly important, and the E-type revolutionized the medium-price sports car market in the Sixties. But the XK-120 introduced Americans to genuine sports cars and did just about everything else besides.

In 1948, for less than $4000, you could buy a roadster with aerodynamic styling that was light-years ahead of the competition. You also got independent front suspension and a double overhead cam 160 hp Six of 3.5-liters with lots of alloy in its castings and seven main bearings. The engine design was the work of William Heynes and Harry Weslake, the dean of British engineers.

The first XK-120s were good for 120 mph, and later ones got up to nearly 140 mph in reworked trim. At the time, Cadillacs—which also boasted 160 hp from a new V-8—were lucky to reach 100 mph. XK-120s were raced, rallied, modified and—more recently—restored. A perfect one will cost considerably more now than it did when new, but examples in moderate condition can still be found for under $2000. Which, as the men from Jaguar in Coventry are fond of saying, is "good value for money."

Lancia

Lancia cars have always been noted for unusual and progressive engineering. For example, unit construction and independent front suspension appeared on the famous Lambda as early as 1922. But Lancia's zenith came in the early Fifties, when it built everything from sedans to Formula One contenders.

The best all-around street model of the bunch is probably the Aurelia B.20, introduced in 1951. This started with a 1991cc V-6 of 75 hp, an unusual sliding kingpin independent front suspension and a transmission in unit with the rear axle. In 1953 the engine was enlarged to 2451cc and 118hp, and in 1954 a De Dion rear axle was installed. The elegant B.20 then remained in production without change until 1959.

The unit body—designed by Pininfarina—was recognized as a landmark in its day, and was exhibited at the Museum of Modern Art in 1953. The B.20 was also a highly successful competition car, winning the Monte Carlo rally outright in 1954 and placing well in everything from the Carrera PanAmericana to Le Mans. There can be no more exciting small Grand Touring car to own.

1958 Lancia Aurelia B.20S / Courtesy George Drum

1967 Lancia Fulvia Sport Zagato / Courtesy Richard C. Crater

The equivalent of the B.20 from the following decade is the Fulvia Sport, with lightweight aluminum bodywork by Zagato. This tiny front-wheel-drive coupe has a 114 hp V-4 of only 1584cc, but a top end of nearly 120 mph. It will even get 25 miles per gallon while out-cornering anything else its size. The Fulvia Sport will also probably be the last true Lancia street GT, now that Fiat plans to phase out the traditional and respected Lancia name added some years ago to its worldwide holdings.

1972 Maserati Ghibli / Courtesy Gary Strutin

Maserati

Like Ferrari, Rolls-Royce and Morgan, there isn't a Maserati that someone isn't collecting. The very first racing car from the three Maserati brothers appeared in the early Twenties, but only after the sale of the firm to Omer Orsi in 1947 did road-going sports cars join sports racers and Grand Prix machines under the Maserati name.

Probably the finest Maserati intended for street use is the Maserati Ghibli. Only 2400 were created between 1967 and 1972, when production ceased, and they cost about $24,000 each. The double overhead cam aluminum V-8 displaces 4930cc, makes 330 hp, and will propel the Ghibli to an honest 168 mph. Everything else about the car matches the performance, but the best part is the body.

The master of automobile styling during the Sixties was Giorgetto Giugiaro, and the very best Giugiaro body is the Maserati Ghibli coupe. Underneath the side marker lights, hefty bumpers and add-on reflectors, the original lines of the Ghibli can be seen as they came from Giugiaro's pen. Austere, functional, taut—the Ghibli is all of these. It is also the most perfect solution to the problem of automobile design that has yet been built. This alone makes the Ghibli one of the most important cars of the last quarter-century.

Mercedes has the most impressive pedigree of all manufacturers, tracing its origins back to 1882 and Gottlieb Daimler. Mercedes-Benz dates from a corporate affiliation beginning in 1926, and has been responsible for some of the most desirable of all sports cars with the SS and SSK models. In the Thirties, Mercedes dominated Grand Prix racing, and the firm enjoyed a renaissance during the Fifties in both Formula One and sports car construction.

The famous 300 SL Gullwing is the most exciting reminder of that time. In its day, its performance was considered overwhelming for a street machine; compared to modern cars, it is, if anything, even more impressive. The six-cylinder powerplant features a single overhead cam and fuel injection, to provide 250 hp from 2996cc. This

Mercedes-Benz

gives startling performance, with a top speed of nearly 160 mph from a car that weighs under 3000 pounds.

The chassis is one of the first tubular space frames used on a street car—necessitating the unusual gullwings to clear the upper frame rails—and the suspension is independent on all four wheels. The styling derives from the factory racing cars created by engineer Rudi Uhlenhaut and designer Karl Wilfert, and is streamlined, functional and thorough—right down to the flush-mounted aero-dynamically clean taillights.

The 300 SL cost less than $10,000 new. Perfect examples are already worth more than that. There is no more prestigious contemporary classic, and no more impressive car to drive.

1955 Mercedes-Benz 300 SL / Courtesy Martin Alperstein

1946 MG TC / Courtesy Walter Genther

The most famous of Cecil Kimber's many MGs is the TC, which took America by storm beginning in 1947. Although it was not much different from the J2 which first appeared in England in 1932, in America it was a revelation. The TC has only a 1250cc, 55 hp long-stroke pushrod Four, a partly synchromesh 4-speed, rigid front axle, minimal brakes and a top speed not much over seventy. Compared to American cars of the day, however, its road manners and precision steering made it seem like a racing car.

To many enthusiasts, an MG TC is still the definitive sports car. With its rakish lines, jaunty cutaway doors and sweeping fenders, it made us aware of a whole new aesthetic. Moreover, a TC is fun. And that, too, was something missing in America since the Mercer Raceabout. It doesn't matter that the extravagantly long hood covers mostly shins, that the wire wheels are rarely round and that the average Detroit compact can outrun it. The MG TC started a whole nation of car lovers in the proper direction.

Morgans are enchanting. There is something almost magical about the absurd pleasure that Morgan owners derive from their delightfully anachronistic machines. And anachronistic they are. The body of this 1953 Plus-4 "Flat-Rad" is virtually identical to that of the first Morgan four-wheeler from 1936—and equally similar to the present Plus-8. The front suspension of all Morgans has been the same since H.F.S. Morgan drew up the first one in 1910. At that time, however, Morgans had only three wheels, and motorcycle engines.

In the postwar years, the bigger Plus-4s have used Standard engines, and later the 1991cc Four from the Triumph TR-2, changing as the Triumph unit grew through the TR-3 and TR-4. The Plus-4 became the 130 mph Plus-8 in 1966 with the 3.5-liter Rover (nee Buick) aluminum V-8. In addition, a smaller 4/4 model based on various English Ford engines was introduced in 1955.

The most puissant of all Morgans are the aluminum-bodied Super Sports with special engines crafted by Morgan exponent Christopher Lawrence. In limited production from 1960 through '66, these are genuine racers, the most famous winning its class at Le Mans in 1962. Except for the unfortunate Model F three-wheeler of the late Forties, there is no such thing as an unappealing—or uncollectible—Morgan. The problem will be in finding one that doesn't have a formidably high price tag affixed. Or that the owner is willing to part with, even at any price.

Morgan

1953 Morgan Plus-4 / Courtesy John Erickson

Porsche

The Porsche Speedster is a lightweight, inexpensive version of the model 356 that attracts primarily the hardcore fanatics among the Porsche cult. The Speedster appeared late in 1954 and continued in production for almost four years. The definitive configuration came in 1955 with the fitting of a 1582cc version of the aluminum and magnesium Flat-four. This is rated at about 70 hp, and gives the bathtub-shaped roadster a top speed of about 100 mph—chiefly because it weighs only 1700 pounds.

The Speedster was the first popular rear-engine roadster, and although its handling at high speeds can be a dangerous trial to the inexperienced, its dashing styling and spirited performance lured a generation of enthusiasts into its drafty cockpit. It's hard to find an unmodified Speedster, because they're still competitive in SCCA racing and mechanical changes are easily accomplished. Prices have also risen dramatically to meet the demand. But if you have Porsche fever, the Speedster is the only sure cure.

1956 Porsche Speedster / Courtesy Allan Sockol

Rolls-Royce

1959 Rolls-Royce Silver Wraith / Courtesy Vintage Car Store

Prior to 1948, every Rolls—like nearly all worthwhile automobiles—had a coachbuilt body. Postwar conditions made such an expensive luxury impossible, with the inevitable result that a standard Rolls of the Fifties is in no way comparable to a Rolls of the Twenties.

A few coachbuilt models were introduced in the postwar period, primarily because the demand for certain body styles did not warrant tooling up for mass production. The postwar model nearest in demeanor to a prewar Rolls is the Silver Wraith. These appeared in the early Fifties and continued in limited production until 1959, when they were superseded by the Phantom V.

Built by James Young, most Silver Wraiths were seven-passenger limousines, although a few five-passenger touring limousines with divider were produced. Normal superlatives fall short in describing the elegance, silence and luxury of these cars. A twenty-year-old Silver Wraith, even for $20,000, is still a bargain.

1963 Triumph TR-3B / Courtesy Carlo Picciotti

Triumph

The first postwar sporting Triumph was the Triumph 1800, later the 2000. This used the same Vanguard engine as the later cars, going into production right after the war and continuing until 1950. It is more of a boulevard car than the rather demanding TR series, with highly original and rather bulbously pretty lines. An unusual feature is a second windshield, which folds up with the rear rumble seat.

The most typical Triumph is the TR-3. It's a development of the TR-2 which entered production in 1953 using the 1991cc, 90 hp Standard Vanguard engine, Triumph Mayflower suspension and a frame derived from the old Standard Eight. The TR-3 was relatively cheap for a car that would best 100 mph, that was attractive in a rather chunky sort of way, and capable of surprising performance when modified by one of the legion of tuners who sprang up to service enthusiastic Triumph owners.

This 1963 TR-3B is the final configuration before replacement by the TR-4. It exhibits all the charm for which Triumph is popular, and it can be purchased today for surprisingly little. Prices are sure to rise as more collectors realize the important place that the TR-3 occupies in the automotive history of the past two decades.

1949 Triumph 2000 / Courtesy Mary Rakauskas ▶

A turning point for Chevrolet was the introduction of Ed Cole's lightweight 265-cubic-inch V-8 in 1955. This "small-block" engine first appeared in the clean and boxy 1955 Chevy, the ultimate version of which is the luxurious two-door wagon called the Nomad. Patterned after a Corvette-like showcar, some 23,000 Nomads were built between 1955 and 1957. A distinctive, practical collector's car, the Nomad has the added advantage of using running gear remarkably similar to current General Motors offerings. This makes for convenient replacement of mechanical parts at reasonable prices.

The most sporting use of the small-block Chevy engine is, of course, in the Corvette, which appeared in 1953 with the old Blue Flame Six but improved dramatically with the 283 V-8 two years later. Probably the best Corvette of all is the 1963–1967 coupe with its distinctive pointed fastback roof. These Corvettes were raced, rallied, customized and street-driven in all configurations. They were cars particularly in tune with their time, and are still much prized today. Strictly stock examples, not unlike Porsche Speedsters, are nearly impossible to find. Corvette enthusiasts are the sort who make constant improvements to their cars, leaving purist collectors definitely in the minority.

Chevrolet

1964 Corvette / Courtesy Udo Glosch

◄ *1956 Chevrolet Nomad / Courtesy Ken Rajczi*

1973 Camaro / Courtesy Philip Schilling

The equivalent Chevrolet for the following period is not the Corvette Stingray, but the Camaro. Particularly the 1970–1973 configuration. This svelte coupe is one of the most attractive American cars ever designed, and performance enthusiasts could order up to a 350-cubic-inch, 370 hp version of the old small-block V-8 in the Trans-Am oriented Z-28. In styling, performance, handling and appeal, the later Camaros are probably the best production cars that Chevrolet ever built. These refined coupes are true Gran Turismo machines, and finding a perfect one is eminently rewarding.

Like so many other car manufacturers, Chrysler Corporation came out of World War II with no new designs prepared. The 1946–1948 cars were nearly identical to the prewar versions, the only interesting variations being the wood-paneled Town and Country coupes, sedans and convertibles. These were carried over in 1949 and '50 after the first postwar restyle.

This 1950 coupe weighs nearly 4500 pounds, and even a Straight-eight of 324 cubic inches and 135 hp has a hard time propelling it quickly. The padded hardtop is an extremely rare factory option, but the remainder of the car is quite typical—huge, impressive, ornately chromed and ingeniously wooded. Kept in perfect condition, there is no handsomer car than a Town and Country, and for this reason good specimens rarely enter the marketplace.

Chrysler

1950 Chrysler Newport Town and Country / Courtesy Walter Levino

1956 Chrysler 300B / Courtesy Carl Earn

In 1955, Chrysler started the 300 series, named for the 300 hp, 331-cubic-inch V-8 with which the big coupes were fitted—the most powerful engines then available in America. The famous Keikfeiffer Chryslers dominated stock car racing that year, and popular acceptance led to a run of 7400 Chrysler 300s built from 1955 to 1960.

The nameplate continues to this day as merely another Chrysler model, but for the first five years, the 300 was a genuine 140 mph American GT. It could be had for a base price of just over $4000, and in the hands of a skillful driver could outrun almost anything on the road. There is a growing Chrysler 300 owner's club, values are rising and good examples are becoming harder and harder to find.

Almost every Ford model is being collected by somebody. But in the past two decades the most influential Ford street machine has been the Thunderbird. Ford invented the term "personal car" when the first of these two-seaters appeared in 1955, and adhered to the concept when applied to a vastly different and far less interesting Thunderbird with four seats in 1958.

In the three years of the two-seater, fewer than 50,000 were built. It came with a bored-out Mercury V-8 of 292 cubic inches, rated at just under 200 hp. In a rather hefty 3000-pound car, this provides decent, if not exciting, performance. By comparison with its direct rival Corvette, the Thunderbird is a much softer boulevard car with an orientation toward silent luxury rather than racetrack performance. At a base price of about $3000, it was also a bargain. Perfect examples can cost double that figure today, and even average specimens have lost very little dollar value over twenty years.

Ford

1957 Ford Thunderbird / Courtesy Francis Maffucci

Hudson

Hudson began making cars in 1909 under the guidance of Roy D. Chapin. During the Twenties they were extremely popular, but declined in the next decade. By the time 1948 brought the first post-war redesign, Hudson was merely another struggling independent, soon to merge with Nash and disappear as a nameplate in 1957. From 1948 to 1954, however, Hudson built some of the most admired cars in America. The "stepdown" Hudson designed by Frank Spring appeared in 1948, and continued basically without change. This has the rear wheels *inside* the frame rails, unit body construction and coil-spring independent front suspension.

For 1951, the famous 145 hp, 308-cubic-inch Six arrived, along with the first "6 = 8" T-shirts. Marshall Teague, Herb Thomas, Dick Rathmann and the Flock brothers began their four-year romp through AAA and NASCAR racing. Twin-H power won six national championships in the two sanctioning bodies. On the street, luxurious Hudsons cruised over the landscape, sturdy tanks with a price in the $3500 range. Good ones are still worth well over $2000 today. An active owner's club insures a steady flow of information, parts and appreciation, and keeps alive the Hudson mystique.

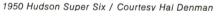

1950 Hudson Super Six / Courtesy Hal Denman

1956 Continental Mark II / Courtesy Francis Maffucci

The Continental Mark II is perhaps the only mass-production car built with the express intention of creating a classic. Happily enough for the Ford Motor Company, it worked. In 1956 and '57, Lincoln shipped 3000 Mark IIs out the door at a list price of $10,000. If the truth be known, few were sold for that much, but the deliberate prestige promotion demanded an exotic price tag.

The Continental is huge. Overall length is 216 inches, and the width is 78 inches. Its 368-cubic-inch V-8 wasn't given a power rating at the time—a Rolls-Royce "adequate" was considered the height of prestige. Ford later admitted to 285 hp, good enough for a timed top speed of 118 mph at Rosamond Dry Lake in 1956.

Clean, austere and perfect, the Continental Mark II still looks contemporary. It's a thoroughly reasonable vehicle to drive and to own except for a chronic defect in the transmission housing (it often cracks, with unfortunate results) and poor power brakes which do little to halt the weighty dowager. But as a collector's object it's hard to beat. Good ones can be had for well under $3000, and that's not bad for a stylish luxury car with one of the best body designs in America, deliberately built to be a classic.

Lincoln

Packard

The greatest of all American marques was founded in 1899. It prospered until after World War II, when Packard found itself unable to switch efficiently from the wartime production of aircraft engines back to automobiles. The firm began a rapid decline, resulting in a merger with Studebaker in 1954 and abandonment of the Packard nameplate in 1958.

From 1952 to 1956, Packard president James Nance tried unsuccessfully to revive the company. The 1953 Caribbean convertible shown here typifies his first superficial efforts to make the older design more contemporary. He was aided by chief stylist Dick Teague, now with American Motors.

The 1953 Caribbean convertible has the rear fenders stretched eight inches to match up with the applied Continental spare tire kit, while the hood receives a wide air scoop. Rear wheel openings are radiused, and Dayton wire wheels are fitted. The rest of the car is

1953 Packard Caribbean / Courtesy James Ragsdale

taken from the standard model, including the 327-cubic-inch Eight. The total is a handsome, very contemporary classic, similar in conception to the 1953 Buick Skylark and Cadillac Eldorado. The automatic transmission is a weak point, but otherwise the Caribbean enjoys excellent reliability—if limited performance—from the proven Straight-eight. Good ones are worth at least $4000—if you can find an owner willing to sell.

1955 Packard 400 / Courtesy Richard Ryan

In 1955, Nance and Teague teamed up for a last-ditch effort. The model 400 shown here is a three-time national Best of Show winner, perhaps the finest postwar Packard in the country. It clearly shows the assertive styling of the Teague era, but the chassis is much more sophisticated than two years previous. The engine is a 260 hp V-8 developed in conjunction with Studebaker, and the chassis features a unique interlinked torsion bar suspension. The 400 is a luxurious— if rather ponderous—example of mid-decade excess. It's a satisfactory car in all respects, built just a little bit too late to preserve Packard fortunes.

In 1965 and 1966, former Le Mans winner Carroll Shelby began modifying Mustang fastbacks into true high-performance Grand Touring cars. This operation was later taken over by Ford itself, and the 1967–1970 Shelbys share only the name. Appropriately named the GT-350, the original Shelby Mustang used the same 289 V-8 as the Mustang, highly modified to deliver anywhere from 306 hp to about 350 hp in full race trim.

Compared to the standard Mustang from which it is derived, the Shelby is lighter, faster, noisier, harsher and tremendously more exciting. Good GT-350s can be had for under $3000 these days. For a handbuilt high-performance GT coupe with a pedigree racing background, that's a bargain like no other.

Shelby's real fame, however, derives from his Cobras, built between 1962 and 1968. These are the highest-performance street cars in the world. They were created initially by dropping 289-cubic-inch

Shelby

1966 Shelby GT-350 / Courtesy Thomas Apuzzo

Ford V-8s into the existing English AC Ace. Later cars shoehorned a mammoth 427-cubic-inch powerplant into the innocent tubular chassis designed to hold a 2-liter AC or Bristol engine.

The original AC was drawn up by John Tojeiro in 1953 and fitted with a replica of the Ferrari 212 Barchetta body. The chassis featured independent suspension on all four wheels, using transverse leaf springs, although Cobras eventually received coil springs at both front and rear. The 427 version, in particular, was a very different car from the relatively tame roadster AC was selling.

1965 Shelby Cobra 289 / Courtesy Carter Gette

A Cobra 289 can do zero to sixty in roughly five seconds and post a top speed of nearly 140 mph. Racing versions are considerably faster yet, while Cobra 427s are not to be believed. Handling is not one of the Cobra's strong points, for so much power in a slightly front-heavy 2200-pound car calls for judicious throttle use indeed. As much a true man's car as anything built since the Thirties, the Cobra is a modern embodiment of vintage motoring in a remarkably inexpensive form. Still, the ultimate 427s are worth well over $10,000 now, and good 289s capture at least $8000.

Studebaker

Raymond Loewy, Virgil Exner and Bob Bourke played various roles in the design of the "double-ended" Studebakers of 1947–1952, with Loewy and Bourke responsible for the landmark 1953 Starliner coupe. This is perhaps the finest postwar American body design of all, the only American car to be included in the 1953 Museum of Modern Art design show. It's cleaner and more contemporary than the classicized Continental Mark II, and completely devoid of the visual legerdemain that characterizes Loewy's later Avanti.

The '53 Starliner, which was powered by either a 170-cubic-inch Six or 233-cubic-inch V-8, did not enjoy performance up to the same standard as the body. But plagued only by chronic rusting problems around the cowl, the Commander Starliner V-8 is still a highly desirable and quite drivable classic of special interest. Overshadowed by later Hawks and Avantis in the eyes of some collectors, good examples can still be found for very reasonable prices. It's inevitable that discriminating collectors will sooner or later discover the Starliner—one of the most perfectly styled cars of the last twenty years.

1953 Studebaker Commander Starliner / Courtesy Gary Lindstrom

1963 Studebaker Avanti / Courtesy Jerry Bowden

The Avanti appeared in 1962, that feverish decade's answer to the '53 Starliner. Created on the 109-inch Lark Daytona chassis, the Loewy design is still valid enough to survive in production in South Bend as the Avanti II. Except that now it has Chevrolet power. As originally produced, the Avanti came with a 289-cubic-inch V-8—later available with a Paxton supercharger from the Studebaker-owned accessory company. Later still, there were 304-cubic-inch versions—supercharged or not.

A genuine 140 mph Grand Tourer, the Avanti was a $4500 bargain in 1962. Good examples can cost nearly that much today. Their front disc brakes, jackrabbit acceleration, decent handling and striking styling make them more than acceptable transportation, and guaranteed collector's items.